Be

Written by Jack Gabolinscy
Illustrated by Raymond McGrath

Harcourt Achieve
Rigby • Saxon • Steck-Vaughn

www.HarcourtAchieve.com
1.800.531.5015

Dad, Ben, and Daren walked up the hill toward the hive. Dad looked like a spaceman in his safety suit and big boots. He carried a large bucket in one hand and a smoker in the other.

"Yummy! Yummy!
I love honey.
Runny honey,
In my tummy,"

Daren sang.

1

When they got to the hive Dad said, “Stand back, boys. It will be hard for me to hear or see you under my head gear if you get hurt.”

Dad puffed smoke over the hive then lifted off the lid. A big cloud of angry bees swarmed around him.

Daren sang:

“Buzzy! Buzzy!
Angry bees.
Puffy! Puffy!
Calm down, please.”

Dad lifted some frames off the beehive. He puffed the smoker carefully and waved the sleepy bees away. He held the frames over the bucket and dropped in the honey.

Ben stared at all the honey. He could already taste it on bread.

Daren started another song.

"Icky! Sticky!
Yellow gold . . ."

"Yeeeooowww!" Ben jumped up and down on the spot.

Dad heard the bees buzzing. He thought Ben was jumping with excitement.

A large, angry bee buzzed on Ben's eyelid. Its stinger was stuck inside his skin.

"Stop moving! Stand still!" Daren shouted.

Quickly, Daren pulled the bee off Ben's eye. He threw it on the ground and stamped it with his shoe. "The stinger's out," he said.

Ben was crying. Daren put his arm around him. "It will stop hurting soon," he said.

The bucket was full of yellow honey. But Dad had no idea Ben was hurt!

"It's still sore," cried Ben.

Daren ran to the water trough and wet his handkerchief. He put it onto Ben's eye.

Ben held the wet handkerchief to his eye and watched his father working.

Daren started a song about Ben's bee sting.

"Bee got angry.
Bee got mad.
Bee stung Ben
And made him sad."

"It's still sore," said Ben. "It's swelling up."

When Daren looked at Ben's eyelid, he got frightened. It was puffed up and Ben's face was going red. Daren tugged on Dad's safety suit. "Come on," he said. "Let's go and show Mom."

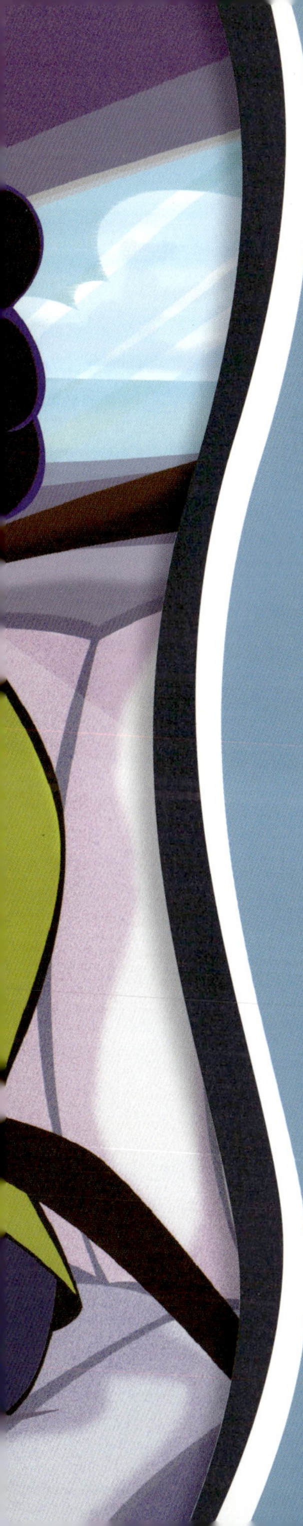

By the time Dad and the boys got home, it was hard to see Ben's right eye.

It was an hour's drive to town. Dad drove like the end of the world was coming.

Mom sat with a wet towel wrapped around Ben's head. "Don't worry! It's only a bee sting," she kept saying.

By the time they got to town, Ben's face was big, lumpy, and red and his right eye had disappeared.

"My face feels like it's on fire," groaned Ben.

The doctor took one look at Ben's face. "He's a very sick boy," he said. "Do I have your permission to give him an injection?"

"Yes! Yes!" said Mom and Dad together. "Just make him well."

The injection stopped the swelling from getting worse, but it didn't make it go down. Ben still couldn't see out of one eye and his face still burned like he was on fire.

"Ben will be OK," said the doctor. "But he needs to stay in the hospital until the swelling goes down."

Ben loved being in the hospital. He got lots of visitors and presents. The nurses read him stories and fed him ice cream. At the end of the week, his face was better and he went home.

Get
Well

Daren gave him a card as
a coming-home present.

It read:

My Bro Ben,
His face got fat.
I'm very glad
He didn't stay like that.

xxx Daren

ELCOME
MY BRO BEN
HIS FACE GOT FAT
I'M VERY GLAD
STAY LIKE

Narratives

A narrative is a story that has a plot (or storyline) with:

An introduction

↓

A problem

↓

A solution

How to Write a Narrative

Step One Write an introduction

An introduction tells the reader:

- Who the story is about (the characters)
- Where the story is set (the setting)
- When the story happened

Step Two Write about the problem

Tell the reader about:

- The events of the story and the problems that the main characters meet
- What the characters do about the problem

My face is swelling up!

Step Three Write about the solution

Tell the reader how the problem is solved.

Don't forget!

A narrative can have more than one main character and other characters.

We are the main characters.

We are the other characters.

Guide Notes

Title: Bee Sting!
Stage: Fluency (2)

Text Form: Narrative
Approach: Guided Reading
Processes: Thinking Critically, Exploring Language, Processing Information
Written and Visual Focus: Illustrative Text

Thinking Critically

(sample questions)

- What do you think this story could be about? Look at the title and discuss.
- Look at the cover. Why do you think the boy looks worried?
- Look at pages 2-3. Why do you think Dad has a safety suit on and the kids don't?
- Look at pages 4-5. Why do you think the smoke makes the bees sleepy?
- Look at pages 6-7. How do you know that Daren wasn't scared of the bee?
- Look at pages 10-11. How do you know that Dad was worried about Ben's eye?
- Look at pages 12-13. Why do you think the doctor wanted to give Ben an injection right away?
- Look at pages 16-17. How do you think Ben felt when he read the card from Daren? Why do you think this?

Exploring Language

Terminology

Title, cover, illustrations, author, illustrator

Vocabulary

Clarify: hive, smoker, honey, trough, permission, swarmed
Nouns: spaceman, bucket, hive, injection, tummy
Verbs: rushed, swarmed, drove, walked, puffed, stamped
Singular/plural: spaceman/spacemen, boot/boots, visitor/visitors
Simile: Dad drove like the end of the world was coming

Print Conventions

Apostrophes – possessives (Ben's eyelid, hour's drive), contractions (stinger's, it's, don't, he's, didn't)